THE PALE INDIAN

By M.C. Laney

 www.trafford.com

North America & international
toll-free: 1 888 232 4444 (USA & Canada)
phone: 250 383 6864 ♦ fax: 250 383 6804 ♦ email: info@trafford.com

FOREWORD

This book is called The Pale Indian. I am one quarter Abenaki by blood. If you don't know who the Abenaki are that's all right, they are fairly obscure. They are part of the Algonquin language group, and lived in the northeast before having their asses handed to them by the English, and having to move north to what is now Quebec. I won't get into a history lesson here, you can find that somewhere else; suffice it to say, they were decimated by disease and war just like most natives in the 17th, 18th and 19th centuries.

I thought it would be appropriate to name the book The Pale Indian because I am one; I am mostly white, and in fact think of myself as white. I am however interested in history, and what my ancestors had to do with it. I find myself more drawn to my Indian ancestry than my white ancestry, as they were the ancestors who had the most difficult struggle of all, that of the white colonization of their lands.

Now I'm not going to go off and start an Indian war or something, I don't subscribe to the Indian way that much. The whites won the war a long time ago, and there is nothing I can do about it. But I can write, and I can criticize, and I can satirize my society; mind you I don't think this society is completely wrong, but there are some crazy people and ideas out there.

If you think this book is going to have a lot of Native American poems in it you are wrong. It's true there are some red poems sprinkled in the book, but the majority of poems are American style. I am American, and I grew up American; I never had anyone give me shit about my Indian heritage, and I am white enough so that no one ever knew about my Indian blood unless I told them.

I think my Indian blood is prominent in my daily life. I am a simple man, I don't like technology, but I have adapted to it quite well. I own a cell phone, but I never use it, I only have it for emergencies. I write on a computer, and that's pretty much all I do on it, except for research. I don't need very much: a car, a place, my cell phone for emergencies, and my computer; everything else is a distraction, and therefore, a waste of time.

So much has changed since my ancestors were alive. We drive ourselves crazy with our hectic lives; how many gadgets do you need to be happy? I don't have anything against gadgets, but they have to be useful, if it's not useful then it's a liability to your peace of mind. Peace of mind is what I am after. I need the simplicity of the "Savage" in order to survive; a hectic job and life would cause me to have a heart attack.

The wisdom of the Indian is what I search for, I don't need pride in my ancestry, (although I do have *a little*), I don't need to protest at a rally, I don't chant "Red Power"; the wisdom of the Indian is my goal, introspection is my path, writing is my way.

M.C. Laney

INTRODUCTION

These poems represent about four years of accumulated work from around 2004 to 2008, with the exception being the title poem, and a few others. I think it is interesting to notice the progression of my writing from the beginning to the end, and even though a few poems were moved around for aesthetic purposes, including the title poem, they are loosely in chronological order. I was writing well before 2004 but many of those writings will never see the light of day; (unfortunately some already have), the majority are turds and deserve to be buried in the ground where they belong. It took a long time before my poems started to get good, and it took longer for me to find my 'voice' or 'style', and I'm still refining it; I suspect it will be a never-ending process.

It is up to you to decide if my writings are good or not. I only hope that inspiration can be gained; a momentary flash of insight or understanding, a cascade of different thoughts brought together by creativity; brought to life with words. I hope that I have sufficiently "charged the words" as Ezra Pound put it; (he meant like electricity), and I leave that judgment up to you.

To the Following who published me:
Zygote in my Coffee
Remark #43

Thank You.

THE PALE INDIAN

My Indian skin is pale
My Indian spirit broken
My white ancestors win
My Abenaki spirit
Floats within a dream of what once was
My Abenaki spirit
Lies like ashes in the fire pit
Of what once was
Where a wigwam once stood
But now my mother and her kin
Stand where wind and shadows meet
And burn within the fire pit
The totem of the Abenaki
A warrior proud and strong
Carved in golden wood
The wood will not burn
It will never burn
But my mother and her brothers
And her sisters stand
Around where the wigwam once stood
And cry into the ashes
Of the cold fire pit

THE BANK

I wish other poets would borrow some sorrow from me
They can take as much as they want
I have plenty from the past
I have made a run on the bank of sadness
And there is no more for anyone else
They should thank me really
But once I relieve my post
What a headache they will have then
For all the sorrow and sadness I take
Will be deposited once again
And black will be the sun and moon
And dark will be the windy storm
And colors will not be quite as bright
When the world hits the bottom
At the bottom you will see my tracks
Leading up the hill of insanity
There at the top of the hill you will find me
Lying on the grass with eyes arched to the sky
Looking at clouds and guessing what they are
And though I am awake
You will not wake me
You will be like a dream to me
…A memory of sorrow and sadness

GOOD THINGS COME TO THOSE WHO WAIT

I smell the teen skin and the goose bumps are stinging my eyes
If only you were a little older than you are now
Or me a little younger

To be that young again when all is fresh and new
And dew on the petals is honey for the soul of a caged animal
With his eyes full of hunger

Who new that we would share all that I fantasized
But it took eight years of growth on both sides for the dream
To come true and the lust realized

My how you grew in eight years and your breasts were like tears
In the eyes of a priest who goes to his death
Not knowing the taste

My how the little girl that I once new could do all the things
That a woman can do in a room lit by candlelight
Fire and glow

Nineteen is a good year I think to myself, as I smell the teen skin
That I always wanted to smell and caress the goose bumps
With leathery hand

And I don't feel guilty for thinking those thoughts in the past
For I waited and waited for your love at last
Instead of taking the bait those eight years ago

THE LIGHT

The dying light of life has hovered its last time over my head
If I don't grasp it with webbed hands it will fade in the air
And I will be dead
How have I come to this?
My life has been mediocre and stale
Except for a few speed bumps along the way
That is when life and light live the most
That is when the moment is as important as anything
When the first time has gone forever
And monotony takes hold
Remember to think in the moment
And hold on to that childish thought
Take the moment and live
Grasp and hold with little child hands
Look but don't see the gritty reality
But accept it instead as trashy beauty all its own
Listen but don't be swayed by boogie men
Be swayed by your own heart instead
Care but don't be bloody and unfair with her heart
Care all the way until it hurts
Fly like a mist before the eyes of the old
Sing like a child that has no worries or fears
Die when it is over and not before
Die with a heart full of gold

THE ARROW

The arrow has blood on it
The scalp has a receding hairline
The club has a painting on it
Blood and a war painting
And so does the Indian's face
He looks at the thing at his feet
It was alive and well just before
But now it grows cold
White man keeps invading
They will never stop
Arrows will not win this war
Red man will have no peace
Red man is fighting whenever
They come to close
More arrows will have to be made
More war clubs and knives
To steal the receding hair
Of the white man

INSPIRED BY BAUHAUS

Shoot me out this dying birth
And clot my bloody vine
Slap me on the ass and cut
The cord of crimson wine
Cradle careful my slimy head
(Bella Lugosi's dead)
Wrap my clammy skin
With Martha Stewart's towel
And shove my crying carcass
Into a plastic prison bin
Give me nipple pointed up
That I may have my last meal
Wait until I'm fed
(Undead, undead, undead)
Wait until I can't feel
To see if my blood is red

SOMETIMES I DREAM OF BEING DEAD

Sometimes I dream of being dead
I see my clammy corpse
Inside a dark coffin
My head is full of worms
There is no movement
There is no sound
But if I listen closely
The sounds of decay become clear
A tiny scratching
The maggots drilling for their dinner
And if I listen closely
I hear the pounding, stomping
Of the living
Six feet overhead

OUT OF BODY EXPERIENCE

Sometimes I find myself outside of my head
I see myself small and worried under the covers
I see the world as others see it, as others see me
The darkness squeezes in on all sides
Soon I will be asleep and dream of better things
But until then I see myself, and I don't like what I see
I see the darkness closing in.

MOCKING MODERN POETRY

I walked
Down the street
And bumped into the man
"How about some drugs" he asked
"No thanks" I said
He stomped his cigarette
Into the ground
And blew smoke
    Into
        My
           Face
I stifled a cough
And thought "what an asshole"
But
I kept waking
Down the street
Looking down
At my feet
At wet cement
And I step
On a crack
I forgot
What was that supposed to mean?
And then I—
ZZZZZZzzzzzzzz

It took me 1 minute to type this shit

DEAD WORDS

Dead people writing dead words
That the living can sometimes read
All they write is dead and gray
Gray like skin that is newly shed
From a lizard or a snake
Gray like a corpse that is newly dead
All empty inside from the maggots
Drilling and boring under gray skin
Empty people writing empty words
That the complete can sometimes read
All they write is empty and sad
Sad like a shadow of death
That hovers over old men
Sad like a regretful last breath
That hovers and finally floats in the air
And covers the sun from despair

THE MEANING OF LIFE

Thinking about this
Will only make you crazy
No one knows but God

THE LIBERATION OF IRAQ

The veil comes down
The Burqa falls to the ground
She is dark and beautiful
Not ugly like you'd think
The men lie in a naked line
Waiting for their turn
She goes to each
And works herself
Into a frenzy
And then the coming starts
The white flows like a river
Tank tread deep
Through the streets
Of Baghdad

LET ME EMBRACE YOU

Let me embrace you
And keep you from the wind
Let the sun fall on your skin
And warm you despite the cold
Despite the lonely world
Let the eyes of innocence look upon you
And love you with reverence
Let my arms wrap around you
And squeeze our hearts together
Let our lips find each other
Despite what others say
And find what others only dream about
Let my hands caress away the tired day
From tired shoulders or worried back
Let my whispered words
Take you to a place of bliss
Let the sun shine through us
And warm our hearts from within

THIS IS HOW I FEEL

This is how I feel
When you talk about him
(I would give my left nut
To be him for one night)
But back to the feeling:
A dying tree with bark peeling
Is standing green less
A gash has opened
Tearing a silent tear
From the top to the bottom
Darkness keeps itself inside
Welling up like tears
That is how my heart feels
When you talk about him

TRUST IN ME

Don't take what other's say to heart
Listen to your own voice
If you don't give me your hand
And your heart and mind
There will be a black spot on my heart
Burned and scorched by the sun
With magnifying glass in hand
You will burn me
A smelly smoke would rise to you
And disappear in the wind
It would be a shame for you
You would not see how loved you'd be
You would not feel my adoration
You would not feel my lust
And happily you would go on
Without knowing these things
And sadly I would go on
With the memories of dreams
Of how good it could be

I STAY

I feel her wild thighs with my dirty old hands
I smell her canyon licorice wet new folded lips
I eat her confidence and her skin a golden tan
I praise her open eyes with my timid glance
I lick the droplets of manna from her sweaty back
I kiss the worries away with someone else's lips
I hide my shy and lonely heart within the crusty hole
I slide my gritty hand up and down with fire fingertips
I breathe her gasp of ecstasy like I just popped up for air
I listen to the sound of bliss and store the memories away
I stay when all the sweat is done and heart is calm again

PEOPLE OF THE DAWN

People of the Dawn
Do not forget
Do not fade away or forget
Those cold winter days
When white men turned you out
Of where you lived before
Your fire pit is cold and gray
Your wigwam is packed away
Your feet are freezing blue
While you walk a blue bird flies
It glides low across your path
To the white man he is to be shot at
To you he is a good omen
The Spirit is always with you
People of the Dawn
There in the north you settled
Where old women weave
Their sweet-grass baskets
Where young red girls
Learn how to be white
And leave their homes
For white man husbands

LOVE IS WAR

Love is war
There is no lack of love these days
There is no sun,
It has turned black as sackcloth
The blood runs down my arm
Into the open mouth of a child
(Feeding is such a nuisance)
The brimstone burns my feet
I slip on my melted sole and fall
There is no moon,
It has turned red as blood
The reddish light comes to me
Down into the pit where I landed
It bathes me in a bloody glow
The hairy spider bites my toe
There is no pain
It scampers off with my toe
To its nest, to feed
At least something got what it wanted
In this dismal place

BEAUTY

There is a song that goes:
Everyone is beautiful in they're own way.
But they don't realize the truth of it:
Everyone is ugly in they're own way too.
While I wile away my days on earth
I think about beauty
I see the ugliness in you
The beauty is brown
The ugly truth screams in my ear
But I can't hear
There is a saying that goes:
Beauty is in the eye of the beholder
But ugly must be in the eye too
If you follow my logic
Than all we need is someone
That believes our lie
And sees without hearing the truth

TRADE IN

She said she would trade in her boyfriend
Because he didn't give her flowers
Well I'll be a flower buying fool if that is what she wants
I'll be a florist's worst nightmare for her
Her office would turn into an endangered animal habitat
That no one could touch
Her heart would be touched, and that is all that matters
Attention to detail is all she is asking for
Someone who will see a flower in the store
And think of her
It would be a small price to pay
And many men I know would gladly pay it
But time eats away these cute endearing things
And more jaded things appear
And then when a year or two have past
And I never buy her flowers anymore
She will trade me in for another flower buying fool

A FIT OF LUNACY

A fit of lunacy has taken me today
I think of what is true and what is false I believe in
I think of all the things that are what ifs and should have done
I think of what she is doing right now
Is she enjoying the company of a friend?
And does that friend happen to be a male?
I think of what others never think about
Or if they do
They let it pass and do not dwell on it
I dwell on it
I build a house of sadness brick by brick
I smear the mortar of madness between every row
I build this house with no doors or windows
There is no way out
I build the walls around me until the light is gone
And still I build on
But there is one thing that will batter the old bricks down
That is the truth
Truth will make a pile of lost hope and regret out of my house
And later
When I get better
I will be thankful for it

PALE

Pale white skin soft to the touch
Eyes blue bright like water wanting
Staring; saying nothing
Thinking everything
An angel on earth
On earth as she is in heaven
Can old lips whisper beware to young hearts?
Everything wanting in the dark
I see in the light covered
Hidden from despair
Hidden from regret
Tied back red brown hair
Reveals her pale neck
To the sun of day
The sun of day gets a peek
The skin burns pink
Nothing anyone can say
Could tell me different
There is nothing more beautiful
Than you are right now

YOU'RE LIGHT

Your light shines out of you
I savor the golden light
It throws my shadow on the wall
A silhouette next to the door

You blind me with your beauty
You steal my sight, my breath
And happily I give it
And still I want to see more

Your light shines through me now
The shadow on the wall is gone
I am like a lonely soul
And something like the sun shines through me

THIS IS LOVE

Love is like walking through fire
It burns the skin
Every inch: on fire
But love, like Novocain
Numbs us; dead nerves
Let us enjoy the pain
Drunken eyes see roses
Warm lips feel moist touches

Love is like a dying man's last breath
Floating, free, weightless
Without attachments
Hurting those left behind
And the sunshine
Like liquid gold
Shines through it
Showing no shadow

Love is an insane thing
Ripping reason
Leaving trails, scars
Of broken footsteps
Across the heart
Toward a trap
And I walk toward it
Eyes wide open

DESIRE

The curve of her hip as it slides along tan lines
The tan of her skin would be perfect for hungry lips
The goose bumps that cover the softness
The peach fuzz that covers the silk
The lips that caress her skin with moist touches
Are the luckiest lips in life
The hands that caress the tan and goose bumps
Are envied by many men
The lips that kiss her lips
Live the story that most would love to tell
The love that her body can give and give up
Is like being in heaven without being dead
The eyes that look deep in her eyes
Are the eyes that see the simple love
The hair that falls on soft bodies and naked necks
Tickles the nerves like nothing else
The mouth that kisses her soft side handles
Is the mouth that speaks no lie
The tear that falls from her hazel eye
Leaves a painful path on my heart

THE ROAD

I see myself in my rear-view mirror
The road glows with sun waves
The clouds roll in
The storm will be here soon
I am lonely on the road
Glassy eyes of flat road kill
Stare into the distance
I can smell the yellow line
Headlights flashing, passing
On the path ahead
Leaving me in the dust
Blinking overhead I see
A Vulture circles, I say-
'I'm not dead yet my friend'
He croaks in raspy response
Landing on a telephone pole
I can see his beady eyes
Sizing up his meal of maggots
And red meat
My feet struggle to keep stepping
Tripping on pebbles, I can't help thinking
If I fall, at least one of us will be happy

MAUD GONNE

You are my Maud Gonne
My unattainable beauty
But a grain of hope remains
A grain of hope is all it takes
To tear a man in two
To lift him up above the clouds
Or lingering on and on
Like William Butler Yeats for Gonne
And if that moment ever comes
When we meet and night is ours
Will our reality
Make the sign of the cross
Over my dead idea of love?

THE STAIRS

Stepping up the stairs
Clutching tightly to the rail
Whispered words of wisdom:
Death to the perfect,
Long life for the flawed

Stepping on the landing
Standing; staring,
At portraits on the wall
Of dead people painted
A long, long time ago

Rain upon the rooftop overhead
Wind upon the window
There is no end to it
Staring; forever,
At dead faces on the wall

OUT OF BODY INEXPERIENCE

I am lost, and nothing is the same, and nothing is the same
Waiting patiently for the next big thing
As I look at myself from outside, from a point in space
The darkness surrounds me, and I sleep in its embrace
The void is kept at bay by soft light from above
I recede back farther into space, my sleeping form shrinking
I pass a million worlds but still keep myself in view
I am as far away from myself as I can be
I see myself as others see me, all my strangeness laid bare
And still the universe expands with each intake of breath
And contracts when I exhale
Sounds in the shadow come from the end of everything
They are late to my ears, but new to my mind
And I still haven't started to ponder the big question:
Am I here or am I there?

REMEMBER

Remember all that you know
It is the doom of men that they forget
Reaching back to days and times
When you knew what it was and how to get it
Forgotten words and looks and guts
When you know it you don't know
It's like taking the first steps on your way to the moon
It looks like its never getting nearer
No matter how far your feet travel
In each moment there is no realization of the past
After each step you look back with pride
To see how far you've traveled
False pride of a false prophet of footsteps
Telling yourself you've done well
Lying and believing at the same time
Pushing the truth away and silencing it

CONFESSIONS OF A SKELETON

Smallpox riddled bodies of my ancestors
Creeping from the moldy ground
Crab grass clogging their mouths
Mud and dirt mingling with their bones
Faded feathers of mighty birds clinging to their heads
They tell a terrible story of hardship native style
Murder of the red man, murder of the whites
The never-ending cycle of human nature
To meet hate with hate and retribution made reality
Until there is no one left to kill or be killed
Crumbs of dirt fall from their jaws as they tell
Of sorrows and hardships and wailing women
No consolation for those left behind
Now their mud clogged sockets grow weary
Eyes that see much more than us grow tired
And the skeletons of my ancestors go back to the ground
Just in time for the ground to be broken
By the new mixed blood Indians as they mash the earth
And build their casino upon the blood of warriors

FUN WITH STICKS

How many of us old men
Whether learned, stately, or simple
In our youth, in "olden times"
Have taken a stick
Some branch from the ground
And with it menaced some girl
Or our friends, who will run from it
Because we dipped the end in poo?

JUST MEMORIES

In the cold dark of night
In the twilight silence
I lie in bed thinking
Of you in the sun
The ringing in my ears
Is all I hear tonight
The rage of blood rushing
…And after
The smile that greets me in the mirror
Just memories in the dark
Street light from the lamp
Creeps in through drawn curtains
Thinking of you in candlelight
Golden skin warm and glowing
Light frame pressing me into the bed
Shadows meeting in the middle
Water dripping in the damp night
Lonely dog barking in the distance
And in the cold dark
As if it were yesterday
I can still feel you brown hair
Tickling my nose.

MANIMAL

How can they do it?
These callous ones
Sizing up another like the predator and his meal
Giving nothing but death
Thinking nothing about giving it
No conscience given to the crying
No mercy given to the living
Heart turned black and cold like a cadaver
Mind turned gray as corpse skin
Feeling nothing but the gun metal in their hand
They pull the trigger, without remorse
And send their victims, bloody, to the afterlife
And they have no choice but to go

COFFEE

Corporate coffee in my hand
I go forth to do your bidding
Unwitting participant of the system
With dollar bill sings in my eyes
Un-free and unwilling to change

One day I go to the show
See the band up close
And in the front row
Revelation and religion mixing
In a moment of euphoria and hope

Somewhere out there in the mist
People do what they like
People do what they're told
I have a vision of life not like the rest
And for that I've been called crazy

But a deep-seated fear creeps into my bones
From years of your conditioning
I feel the need to buy Starbucks coffee
Plasma TV's and pretty cars
Get drunk at all the bars and take someone home
At the crossroads I pause to think
Like the Talking Heads said:
"How did I get here?"
Now I find out that I am still a drone
All I did was change to a different system

HAVE MERCY

Bow your head; my little angel, and pray for me
Ask Him to forgive and to forget
As we forget those who trespass into and out of our lives
Forgive me if I forget the lessons of the past
And help me to remember the good times and lessons taught

Forgive those who take me for granted
Let them see what they have missed
Let them see how I would have loved them
Let them see that what they know is the tip of the iceberg

Ask Him for me; my little angel, ask him to melt me
There is no opening without first being closed
There is no look without eyes first being shut
Light shines through shut eyelid
Through skin and blood shows red
The door stands ajar with gray knowledge behind

Smokey and soft the mannequin beckons

WIND BLOWING THROUGH MY HAIR

All that I am
All that I will ever be
I give to you

Wind blowing through my hair
Falling from the building
Suicides are rare

All that I am
All that I will ever be
I throw at you

UNTITLED

As I harvest the dandruff under my fingernails
I ponder power lines outside my window
House upon house, block upon block
And still the power surges through the lines
Inside tepid people gaze into PC's
Or sit like protuberances upon the sofa
Staring mindlessly at the TV
Some flare-up in the Middle East, a shit hole anyways
Or maybe a reality show, a shit hole anyways
Yesterday I saw through the power lines
Saw the hills and trees behind them
Saw the rift in between buttock like hills
Imagined a little stream in between
Where only Indians and homeless have been
Right there, a long time ago, there was the old Mission
Flattened by the earthquake long ago
Cut through with the trough of railroad and spikes
Coming back to reality, is see the black wires again
As I sit here in front of this screen
I ponder where the power goes

UNREQUITED LOVE

I sit here in my idiocy, crying
And me wrapped up with my pretentious writing
How can I buy you all the things that you hold dear?
I have my Ipod; I have my corporate coffee
I have my unemployment; I have your friendship
How can I buy you all the things that you hold dear?
I sit here in my idiocy, thinking
And you wrapped up with all you living
How many men have cherished your body?
How many men have thrown you away?
How many men have loved your lovely lips
And not your filthy mind?
But I loved your filthy soul
Before I touched your silky skin
And then you slapped my hand away
Angry and indignant
I am not welcome
But they are, aren't they?
You just don't know how much that hurts

ONE TIME

One time when I was drunk
I fell to the ground at night
I smelled the dark grass
I felt the cold dew between my fingers
But then the earth began to tilt
And I was like a spider, clinging
To a grass wall
Then it tilted upside down
And I prayed to God:
Please God; don't let me fall
Don't let me fall into the sky

I LOVED HER

I loved her too much, and she grew tired
Of my infant mortality rate
Any more mortality and she would have died
As our love died and transitioned
Into the bloody sore of friendship
A bloody sore, weeping pain
A dirty disengaging that I wanted no part of
Especially when she found a new friend
And turned the page on me
Like a sullen child reading over her shoulder
Not yet done but forced to start another page
The umbilical cord was cut
Without anesthesia
I don't blame her for giving birth
I blame her for listening to others
How can they know more about us than we do?
And taking their advice instead of ours
She turned her heart against me
Yet she would have turned her heart eventually
I know that now
But maybe, if not for them,
we would have had
A little more time together than we had
As I write this I feel no pain
So much time has passed
I am objective, truth seeking
Numb and all knowing

OCTOBER 2001

It was October 2001; I was at the Midnight Oil show
Hollywood House of Blues
After 9/11 not too many people were in the mood for dancing
The usual freaky people were there, and me too
Some of them probably never heard of the Oils
We were all stunned, we were all wary
We were all told to go on living our lives as usual
Or the terrorists win
People bobbed their heads to the music, but didn't dance
Peter made his usual politically erudite remarks between songs
And then they played "Hercules"
If you've never heard this song, I urge you to partake my friend
It is one of the most well written songs that was ever made
It rocked us to the core, made us forget
Made us dance again
This is something I will remember...

CHANGE

Change is like being born again and again
Each time we go from what is old to what is new
Change is a chain of wombs stretched out into the past
As we dive into cold life from warm beginnings
Warm and wriggling in the blanket of the dark
Silent sounds come through the airy water
Warm and dark is all we think from hour to hour
Then we go, or are led; from one world to another
From one confined box to the beautiful outside
Clawing our way through the canal
Are we trying to escape or claw our way back in?
Blinking in the bright light
Colors and light wash away the night of the tomb

THE BLAZING LID

From the darkness inside I am hid from all that worries me
Above me the blazing lid beckons to be opened
Staring at the fire and not wanting to be scorched
I cower in the bottom of the pit of my own making
Sometimes I imagine what is outside my prison
All the light, color and gladness that could be mine
The sadness that all the others have to go through
All the time they are alive on the outside of this
Then without thinking I jump and hit the lid
Breaking right on through to the other side
All the light and color stabbing through my eyes
All the gladness, all the madness, all the newness
I run with wild delight, without thought of pain
Until I run into a wall, then I look up again
There, far above, a glow in the sky
The blazing lid beckons me like before

I KILL ME

I want to kill who I am and become who I will be
I want to free myself from this prison of the old
I want to hover over the old me like a spirit
Drifting, seeking, measuring a new time and place
A new heaven is set out before me, like a race
But there is no finish line; there are only deaths and births
And births and deaths, and shadows cast by new suns
I want to do away with the way I once was and am
I want to leave old prejudice behind like the past
I want to leave preconceived notions of who I am
In the trash, where it belongs
The outdated stigma of the artist, of the writer
I want to cover my ears like a child and sing
"I can't hear you; I can't hear you, nyaa nyaaa!"
But I can't can I? I have to stand and fight
Stand and fight for who I want to be
Not what *you* think I should be or want me to be
Not what western thought thinks I should be
Not what a shadow thinks I should be
The shadow has never seen the sun
But the shadow knows its there, waiting;
Just waiting
Beyond the silhouettes of old men

OUTER SPACE

Any night I look up into the vast canopy of the sky
It makes all the petty arguments go away
The problems of one man or woman pale in comparison
To the endless wandering eye that pierces the dark
It sees more than just infinity but infinity is just as good
To teach the forgetful few the lesson to let go of heavy things
What does it matter to the stars and the big empty spaces?
Those places will still be there when you fail to resolve the
　　　　　problems
The problem with problems is that they all pale in comparison
To the empty places; the stars and suns of outer space
Like a grain of sand bothers your big toe at the beach
Or like a butterfly whirling around in a category five hurricane
What does the hurricane care?
What does the big nothing care?
I want to be the sun
Burning with fire for every day's light
The sun doesn't care about your cares; and has no enemies
What does the sun care about petty things that people do?
I want to be the sun
Watching people waving their tiny arms
Making shadows with their bodies and sounds from their
　　　　　mouths
Yelling at each other, hurting each other, fearing each other
Fucking each other, hating each other, killing each other
I am the sun
I burn and watch them until nightfall.

SOMETHING ABOUT DEATH

Heh heh, there is nothing left to say
So I will say something about death
Maggots will burrow into brain box
Skin will wither to the bone
As I lay in my sweaty coffin in the dark
My head resting on the wood
My mouth agape in a silent scream
Above I hear footsteps of the living
The maggots in my ear drown them out
Tomorrow will be more of the same
Flowers grow over cold stone above

TIN FUNNEL

Thousands of wings flutter in my mind
Bearing weight within my skull
Aching, barely not breaking through
My eyes bulging, popping
Red and yellow, brown and blue
I drink a bottle full of tears, quenching
I eat dried heart, tough as jerky
Solemnly I weep through eyeholes
Cravenly I sleep in cancerous bed
Huddled, hiding from everything
Sobbing, wetting, growing wet spot
Half of nothing is all I have
The truth is all I have to leave
I catch my tears with a tin funnel
Replenishing the bottle

REGRET

The tears of regret are dark and full of pain
They roll down the cheek leaving a trail
A broken promise piled high with other promises
In a pile of old promises told to myself

These are the things I wish I would learn:
Learning to cherish family and friends
Family and friends not cherished and gone.

Tears of regret have the bitterest taste
Like rust in the mouth of a mechanical man
Knowing the truth but not doing a thing
Relaxed and lulled into a false sense of security

IDK

Tearing a new one for the old one
As we tear those who trespass against us
Smiling and stabbing at the same time
Hurting and laughing at the same time
Fearing full disclosure of our sins
We take what we can from others
They take what they can from us
We give as little as possible
We give it grudgingly like a jealous child
Sharing a toy with another
We run in the race without knowing why
And fall before the finish line

PESSIMISM (a.k.a. REALISM)

Panting, pausing, lovely death
I will write about my broken heart
Is there anything I can create, anything
That will solve your puny problems?
All this crap I put down, from the heart
It means nothing once you close the book.
All the poets of the world can't help me
No therapist, no father confessor, no time.
My heart is closed inside a wall of red stone
The sweaty bricks pulsing, bulging with each beat
And time is beating the ticks of a clock
What matters what you make, what you say?
Nothing... nothing at all.

FIRST IMPRESSIONS

Take a gander at my wandering soul
What aura, what color do you see?
Declare to me that you don't understand
What shell stops your vision from the truth?
What plastic, what painted outside belies the truth?
Heaven help the ignorant; heaven help me.
I stop at your shell, and that's as far as I get;
I'm no better.
Look into my eyes; see the lies or the truth
Mirror in your eyes the beautiful noose
I see heaven, safe harbor; lighthouse signals
I see somber sadness, thrilling fire
Flowers washed by tears
Heaven help me...I see life

MY WAY

Painting my fears into a corner
Writing my way into a new life
Handling everything with new hands
Crying only when there is a death
Laughing only when there is a life
Smiling at all the ones who call me crazy
Smiling a crazy man smile, why not?
They have a firm grasp on insanity
What they think is good, I think is crazy
What they think is happiness, is not
If they choose to deny, then so be it
I am not one to pass judgment out loud
They do what they have to do
I make a new life with new hands
Stuttering, stumbling and finally free
Mumbling, shouting crazy man dreams

FUCK YOU

Imperfect, bad seed, black sheep
Born under a bad sign
Put me away in a safe for safe keeping
Drag me out into the street before all my neighbors
Convene the hearing; let's hear it
Tell the court what you think
You think you know what's wrong with me?
I've done a terrible thing, a terrible thing
I am not like you.
The crime of the fucking century
Put me on trial, put all the rumors to the test
You can't hurt me anymore
Grasping, sweating, you get nothing from me
…There is nothing to get

ROLE MODEL

He was a sorry teacher
He was terrible with people
I have to believe that I can do better
If I didn't believe
What would be the point of going on?
The point is to improve, solve what he could not
Print the answer in black and white
See? I am better than him
I am not like him, not that way
I am forty times better
I peer down the well at his fat face
I drop the pail on it
Have you drunk from that well?
Have you tasted the fake poison?
Drink what you think is the best water
…Leave the dregs for the grave

DAD

Nodding off at the dinner table
Not from sleepiness; from drunkenness
Cigarette in hand with a column
Of ash that hasn't fallen
Eyelids slowly closing, shutting the world
Dissolving the world in a 40 ounce bottle
Clinking and clanking if his leg twitched
And hit the forest of empties at his feet
I look at my dad with disdain
He's not living
He's looking at the inside of his eyelids
Passing out slowly, passing away slowly
Slowly succumbing to death
I'm just as disappointed in him
As he is of me, as he is of reality
Disgusted and embarrassed at the same time
Let down by my dad
Before anyone else could

ALL TRUTH

I am drained of all truth
I stare at my silhouette on the wall

I dream of a world more precious
More stable than this one
More laughter, more love
More nobility than this one

I dream of a world less worthless
Less chaos than this one
Less crying, less loss
Less spineless than this one

I am awakened by the truth
By the truth we are turned
Instilled with bravery
Freed of all anchors to the past

TAKE MY HAND

Take my hand
Lead me to the promised place
Do the math
All my answers have been wrong
Look at me
I don't conform to all your labels
Stab my heart
Have faith in me or leave me alone
Light my shadow
Show me the precipice of possibilities
Sooth my fears
Dead Herbert said 'fear is the mind killer'
Suck it up
Don't take life so seriously
Haven't you heard?
Death is searching for you always
Hold my heart
In your hands lined with gold leaf
Go to hell
I don't need you is what I keep saying
Shut your mouth
Clouds of gnats always fly at mouth level
Show me bliss
Pull Heaven down and smother me
Wipe my tears
Don't let them fall into the opened ground
Don't judge me
Accept me for who I am, was, and will be

Touch my skin
Don't let me be the only one for too long
Break my heart
There is a beginning, middle, and always an end

LESS THAN FIVE

The smell
The touch
After all this time
I was never more numb than I was then
Memories of my sister's friend's Lava Lamp live in my mind
Like they are still alive, like the day I lived them
Stop! Think of all the missing pieces of pictures
Moving, alive, more alive than this
Memories of my first pussy, my cousin, she showed me
I was scared; I was less than five
I told on her, I saw, and I told, it was hairless
She was scolded by my Aunt, her lips folded in
Just a dark line, nothing showing
Movies of memories of defining moments
Holding my mind to the past, straining to relive
Bitter innocence, why are you so simple?
Halo of golden light surrounds you
Bitter innocence, why are you leaving?
Starving after time, becoming wisdom, dying peace
Heaven is full of the likes of you, or if it isn't
Then why would you want to go there?
Silver innocence, memories of my sincerity
I looked up the old woman's skirt at the store
Varicose veins and grandma panties, panty hose
I was scolded, and I remember not giving a damn
Like I had done nothing wrong
Nothing wrong to revel in my memories of before
I remember when my sister and her husband came to stay

The hideaway bed from the sorry couch
Their bodies pressing into the lattice of wire mesh
I wound my way underneath and pushed up on the bumps
So much that I was scolded again, and laughing
And laughing
I am laughing today, watching the comedy in my mind
In the prehistory before wisdom and morals
At bath time the world is inside a white porcelain tub
Water is a solid thing
With movement and chrome colors
Splashing water out of the rim, scolded again
Making bubbles with body gasses
Floating boats with plastic sides
Watching whirlpools with eyes of lazy angels
Watching everything in the world, all that was lit
And in the shadow beyond did not exist to my mind
The monsters were real to me, they chased my down the hallway
Snapping at my back all the way, until I reached the light
Seeing faces of family and friends
Looking back at darkness
From a safe and secure footing
Saturday morning cartoons
Playing in the puddles after it rains, clouds calling sliding
All the while not noticing the ugliness, the dirt, the shame
The reality of life and loss and pain and tears
Tears are shed over dropped ice cream
Over calamities like toys not shared
Candle light and shadow shining in my eyes
A big wax four lit on a German chocolate cake
All my people singing to me, made me feel shy, guilty

Or my first thunderstorm, and me under the table scared
My dad trying to explain
And though I don't remember what he said, seeing him unafraid
I was unafraid; I was inside an impenetrable place
And sounds
Sounds can crash outside all they want; I was unafraid
Today if I had the chance, I would go there again
I would give all the moments away, the science, the math
The knowledge of things and how they matter
And I would wave goodbye to wisdom with laughter
I would gladly give it up to be less than five again

I WANNA BE A STAR

Killing the soul one reality show at a time
Slipping on the blood of the next action hero
Closing the drapes on the light of the sun
Filling the empty hole one one-hit-wonder at a time
There is no joy in television
There are daggers in the eyes of Hollywood
There are powders and pills on the dresser
How many die this year?
Grasping for brass rings with mummy hands
Riding plastic horses all the way to hell
There is a sinkhole in southern California
Everywhere else people avoid stepping in shit
There is no avoiding it
Money doesn't make the world go 'round
Love of money makes the world go 'round
Will the world stop going 'round
If the movie star passes away?

THOUGHTS ON IRAQ

Enemies at every hour on the hour
Our soldiers have the best equipment in the world
Is the Iraqi kid giving you a flower or a hand grenade?
What's that thing on the side of the road?
Fucking like there's no tomorrow
Killing like there's no today
Laughing at the present situation is the only way
To stay sane in an insane sand box
Giving you're country an arm and a leg
The highest price to pay for freedom is death
I'm glad there are some who would gladly pay it
I'm too much of a pussy to pay it
But I'm glad I won't be going to jail tonight
For writing bad things or good things about the war
That's what they're dying for, for things like freedom of speech
...Dying hero's, every hour on the hour

LOVEWELL'S LAST SCALP HUNT

I will take the Talking Stick, when it is passed
And tell you something about my dreams:
I see red hatchet work for Adeawando
Musket balls silver and screaming through the air
From white muskets and red muskets
Powder clouds thick and foggy
Between the two peoples like morning mist
Powder poured down musket barrels
Powder poured into flash pans
Killing each other like animals
Each side looking for scalps
One side for money, one side for revenge
Grabbing and running knife along hairlines
Peeling and pulling back bloody skin
Men treating men like animals
…Mutilation the measure of a man

FLOWER

Kiss the flower with wet touches and breath
Smell the dew clear in nectar silver drops
Move the lips with movement, motion
Peeking tongue between, seeking something
Tangy and intangible but seeking none the less
Coppery, iron, bloody taste
Sun dimpled flower, sunflower
Clean-shaven toe, soft, so soft and yielding

CHIBAI IN THE NIGHT

The moon shines new light
And leaves new shadows for the warrior
To hide, like a Chibai* in the night
Drifting; floating…silent-intent
Death bringing and dangerous
The scalps of the Awanoch† have little time
Before they are ripped and taken
Without remorse, it's nothing personal
Hair is fair game
When they are at war

* Ghost
† White Man

CLAY FACE

Clay faced Hugo Chavez	[Hugo]
Mr. Potato Head	[Chavez]
He likes power a lot	[Eats]
He likes Socialism too	[Freedom]
The kind where they kill you if you disagree	[With]
The Venezuelan's don't mind	[A]
They follow Clay Face	[Silver]
Gripe and protest; then do nothing	[Spoon]

BONITA

Bonita Maria, you make me sad
You were murdered and buried under the mountain
Tadpoles living in your eyeholes
Worms wriggling in your marrow
Will justice take her blindfold off long enough to see?

Bonita Maria, you make me sad
Tadpole home and worms repast
Resting under blessed mountain
Bloody handed hatchet man not confessing to the crime
When will anyone ever cry over your yellow bones?

Bonita Maria, you make me sad
Maria, you were not a prostitute
They said you ran off with your boyfriend
Your body has not been found
How long will Quetzal let you down, Bonita?

Bonita Maria, you make me sad
Red-handed murderers walk the streets of Guatemala City
You, Maria, walk no more
You, Bonita, are beautiful no more
You walk on paths that only angels tread

BEAUTIFUL N8KSQUA

I want a beautiful N8ksqua* for my own
She will send my tired bones to heaven
With every touch, and every lick
And; walking on stars like hot coals
I will walk the path of the M'teoulin†
Starting with the back of the turtle
Never-ending; somber…smiling
She will walk with me always
With me always Abenaki woman
I am Awanoch
I am seeking something
Without strife, without heartbreak
Your eyes hold the stars in an embrace
Waiting for Awanoch to see them
Waiting for me to be reflected in them

* Maid
† Shaman

SET MY HEART FREE

See my sorry face
I set it with the mortar of delusion
Set God free from this place
Set my heart free
Something in my heart stirs at your embrace
Something stirs
Capture God in a golden cage
Set him free with the key
Give me the key to unlock myself
Free me from this page
Set my spirit free
Kill my Messiah with golden nails
Kill him on a golden tree
Smother my fear with a security blanket
I smother myself with fear
See things in a Chinese way
Accept things in a Chinese way
…The midnight dew is dry by midmorning

I REMEMBER

I remember some summer days when all was well in the world
We climbed up Chalk Mountain back behind Fir Street
We took with us cardboard sleds and climbed the chalk
That stood like a broken knee on the side of the hill
With handholds and footholds carved in by other kids
Then we'd sit on the cardboard and ride the chalk down
To the bottom of the hill where grass broke our fall

I remember Pam from the cul-de-sac; she was nice to me
She taught me how to pick dandelion flowers
And hold them out for bees to land on
She said she had a boyfriend that could lift her car
It was a Beetle and I didn't believe her
And I couldn't understand until later why she stopped
And I had to find a new friend my own age

I remember making cardboard armor with my brother
We made wooden swords with wooden guards nailed on
That cardboard armor didn't stand up to well against them
We ran down the sidewalk fighting our knights' wars
We inspired another boy to make his own armor
But his armor looked like a trash can compared to ours
We laughed until he went away saddened and rejected

NIGHT FIRES

Put out the night fires, put out the sparks
Soon I will sleep again
Dreaming of wigwam nights
Red girls sweating against me
Breaking the silence of the night with soft moans
Sweeping the smoke up the smoke hole
Out into the cold night
Yawning cold night, white night
Put out the night fires, put out the sparks
Dreaming Indian dreams again
Sleeping in furs of dead animals
Cupping her red face in white hands
Kissing her red lips
Caressing her red hips with white hands
Put out the night fires, put out the sparks
Soon we will sleep again
Dreaming Caucasian dreams this time
Dreaming of a lonely white man
Writing dreams down on a computer

OVERCOMPENSATING FOR "SOMETHING"

Tonight the world sleeps a fetid sleep
Tomorrow brings a bright day of dark smoke
And ashes to cover the cowering world

Raping is what the Russian Czar has in store
For small Georgia on this day
Tanks for Tbilisi and dirt for the poor

Putin gives the orders to the puppet
And watches from a distance the action
While dead mothers clutch dead babies

The words of one man are enough to burn the world
The arrogance of one man is enough
To set the world on fire for his vanity

No man is as ugly as Putin; pitiful Putin
No man is as comfortable with insanity
No asshole is as big as Putin's dick is small

Where are the western pinnacles of power?
Their heads are up their asses

BRAVE WINEMA

Brave Winema, Modoc woman
You tried to save them
Weium warned you; true Weium
Soldiers laughed at you
They didn't listen to your wisdom
Because you were a woman
And not a Modoc man
And not a white man
How could they know your bravery?
How could they know your heart?
You saved your man from a bear
Or so the story goes:
The bear was chasing Frank Riddle
The end of his life was near
From out of a cluster of bushes
You surprised the bear shouting
Waving your arms
The bear stopped, ran from you
Not many would stand up to a bear
...If the soldiers knew you better
Maybe they would have taken your words to heart
Maybe they would not have died
At the hands of treacherous Modoc warriors

THANK GOD

I lifted up the covers
Surprise!
She was naked!

Laying on her tummy
Beautiful butt all rounded
Beautiful back dimpled and arched
Goosebumps on white thighs
Smile on her face

Her pale thighs moved like melted ivory
Under my searching hands
Until they reached the middle
(Legs parted slightly)
My fingers were wet with her wetness

What did I do to deserve her?
Thank God for her
Thank God a thousand times for her

HEARING NOTHING

There is nothing as silent, nothing so loud
As the heart beating in between night seconds
Ticking and ticking away
Silent night seconds
Let me listen for a while, straining ears
Grasping any micro vibration
Distant cries
Humming monsters of modern machinery
Sipping power from the lines
Humming nocturnal dreams
Creeping ankle pains remind me
To keep breathing
Counting silent night seconds for the second time
Counting barks of a dog
Something about the silence soothes me
Tranquility soothes me
Soothing to the mind,
Open to any sound

GRAY SHORT SHORTS

I saw her smooth pale thighs and wondered
What would I find behind those gray short
Shorts, would it be shaved, groomed, or bushy

 I would inhale the smell before sliding
Tongue between two lips, tasting honey
Sticky and soft, warm and smooth

Heart beating faster, pounding
Hands roaming up peach fuzzy belly
Cupping warm breast and pinching the nipple

She is waiting at the cash register
I am eating my food and glancing
My tongue makes the moves inside my mouth

That I would love to make on her

THE DAY DIES

The day dies; the night wins
I have seen my ghost today
He walked unhappy into the church
One candle burned for the one who passed away
My eyes watered for myself but I held back
My ghost confronted me, angry
"Mourning a wisp of smoke is no way to live
I am the one who should be mourning you", he said
"If my hands could grasp, I would light a candle for you"
I denied him; I ignored him
People sang, the priest intoned the ritual
But my eyes drifted back to the lone candle
Single flame wavering through watery eyes

SPIRIT TEST

'Go' the grand medicine man said
'To the mountain of insanity and madness
There you will have your vision of wisdom
The spirits will take you by the hand
They will show you the way now
Follow them on the path with a free heart
If they tell you to catch the stars
Then you better have the Power to catch them
If they tell you to stare at the sun
You better not shield your eyes
If they tell you to change your skin
You better have the Power to change it
If you don't have Power
If you don't pass the test
The spirits will throw you down the mountain
And you will hit every rock on the way down
If you cannot awaken your Power
You had better not start up the mountain
Throwing learners down the side is their way'

I HAVE POWER

I pound the drum
And plead with the spirits to come
To my hut and give me the Power
Over flesh and sun and moon and wind

I throw the flesh
On the fire as my song goes higher
And the flesh sizzles and smokes
And goes out the hole at the top of my hut

The dance is complete
The drum sounds no more
As the spirit gives all his Power
And my soul goes out through the door

I thank the spirits
This hour for giving me all their Power
To help and heal and make the rain fall
...But I am a man after all

In walks the Chief's daughter
A slender red girl guided by spirits
'Will it rain tonight?'
I bring her down to the floor:
'...No'

MAGUAS AND METIS

Maguas: when will you teach me, old man,
The Song of Returning?
I have the Power to learn it

Metis: but do you have the will to use it wisely?

Maguas: I have wisdom, and if I didn't
You would not be teaching me
Teach me the song
It is my right to learn it

Metis: there are many things you will never know
It is not your place to know it all
When I was young we had respect
We did not ask such things

Maguas: what about divination?
Reading the entrails of animals?
For what the omens tell us?

Metis: There are many forms of divination
Reading entrails is only one way
There are many ways that I won't teach you
I can: watch the flights of birds
           The way the wind howls through the trees
           The patterns of blood spattering in the dust
           Watching the moon and stars wheeling

Maguas: why, old man, do you withhold from me?
Why not teach me everything?
Why do you hoard your Power?

Metis: I know why you want more Power
I was young once, long ago
You want to impress a woman
You want to show off your Power to win a heart

Maguas: it's true; I seek the hand of Senewa
But what helps me helps the tribe
You should not let Senewa cloud your decision
Leave her out of this, old man
It's better for the tribe to have two medicine men
Instead of just one

Metis: Don't think, young snake, for one minute
That you can talk your way past me
I am the master and I know all talks of deception
All ways of saying things to get what I want
You can't fool a master
It is wrong to seek Power for the wrong reason

Maguas: But I'm ready—

Metis: I will accept only your apology
And all of your tobacco
It's not right you treating me this way
When I was young we had respect
Wanting power to impress a woman

Can only lead to bad things
Do you want to become a Sorcerer?

Maguas: No,
You're right, I'm sorry; it's not my place
To ask what you will teach
Only that I learn what you teach
And use it only when needed
Not to impress Senewa

Metis: that's better
You youngsters should have more respect
Now run off and fetch my tobacco

UNHAPPY GHOST

Unhappy ghost
You haunt me with your life
You taunt me with your death
I don't see you
Electricity touches my lips
The memories of past kisses
That I miss
Happy endorphins from touches
The non-conformity of love
I miss you
All the kisses I could have had
The warmth that passed me by
I mourn you

HOMMAGE TO FRANÇOIS VILLON

I, M.C. Laney
Being of sound mind and body
Do hereby bequeath the following
Upon my eventual demise:

Item to the Catholic Church
I leave my virgin buttocks
Don't tell me what you do
I don't want to know
I have shit my last log
From my hairy asshole
And no longer need it
Holy, holy, holy, Amen.

Item to my Welsh tart
I leave my lips and tongue
Place them on your pussy
Whenever you need a kiss
Bring them back up to your mouth
And taste yourself
I will watch over you
Whenever I pass away

Item to Vladimir Putin I leave my dick
His must be so small
Since he wants so much power
I offer him mine
And though I am an average Joe

It is probably twice his size
He has the money and power
To get it attached

Item to Hugo Chavez I leave my face
A transplant is in order
Like that French chick
Whose dog ate her face off
Ugliness is a thing of the past
And even though I am no star
It is ten times better
Than his ugly face

Item to the $cientologists I leave my brain
You need it more than I do
You are so stupid and dumb
That even my mediocre mind
Can bring you out of darkness
Bring you out of blind belief
It is your stupidity
That makes you beautiful

Item to the creators of South Park
I give you nothing
You have everything you need
Genius and laughter
I think history will show
That you two killed our culture
In the best way possible
Take a kiss on the ass from me

Item to Ward Churchill
I leave my sense of conscience
You have no Indian blood
You don't represent me
Growing your hair long
Will only make me want to scalp you
You should be ashamed of yourself
You vaginal fart of the world

Item to Hip Hop I give my humble talent
You kiss each other's Asses
And give each other facials
Drenching the hip hop "artist"
Forming a gooey white chrysalis
A wrapper for the rapper to mature
Take a lesson from me:
Writing takes a lot of fucking practice

Item to Michael Moore I leave my heart
His has just about had it
He is so fat he farts cholesterol
And has not seen his dick in years
My heart will also give him common sense
Something he and others like him lack
And if he doesn't follow my heart
Then he can go to hell

Item to the United Nations I leave my balls
How many ineffectual resolutions

How many empty threats
Does it take to make you act?
Take my balls and attach them
And even though I am slow like a turtle
Even so it will be ten times faster
Than you are, corrupt U.N.

Item to the soldiers of both wars
In Afghanistan and Iraq
I leave my arms and legs
Getting your shit blown off
To sow the seeds of freedom
In lands where people hate you
Is a sacrifice I can't compete with
…Thank you for your sacrifice

REMEMBERED LOVE

Inspiring all these words: her fingers
A pale hand reaches out from the blue
Soft wrist slightly wrinkled near the palm
Warm and encouraging fingers interlocking
Tremors off the chart, up the spine,
Below the belt
Now you know what love is all about
Encapsulating lovers in an impenetrable place
Where nothing sad can enter
Bad thoughts are suffocated
By a killer high on dope
Your beauty is seen through a beam of sunlight
Through a window
Dust motes in the stream are denied their shadows
No thoughts of the future
No seeing into the future
Souls are as close as two souls can press
In a dream of Utopia
Showing naked bodies to the sun
Showing glowing smiles to the moon
Saving us from the cell
The prison of our own solitude

NEW SLAVERY

The past mocks the new boss
Before the day is out a new slave is born
Unkempt, passive, eager to work and be worked
The white man laughs, pursues higher learning,
Trying to grasp dollars without sweaty labor.
A new immigrant is hired
The white man tells him what to do
And pays him under the table his slave wage
Why is what he does so demeaning America?
Are you afraid of breaking a nail America?
When did pride in labor die?
They're not taking our jobs
They're taking THIER jobs
The jobs our grandfathers used to have sweaty pride in
Today everyone wants to be the boss
But no one wants to be demeaned by being
On the receiving end of an order
Shame on you America
Where is your humility America?
Why are you ashamed to pick up a shovel,
To wash dishes, to build houses, to clean toilets,
To harvest crops, to drive cabs America?
Working harder for less is the American way
Working less for more is the American dream
Now that the recession is here,
What will you do to make ends meet America?
Will you lower yourself down to sweaty labor?

THE POET PLEADS WITH THE GREAT SPIRIT

I sculpt my identity
With your grace and manna
And while I weep about the past
I stare out at the future
I ask only that I have the power
To make imagination
Into timely action
Attraction, position in your universe
A place of non conforming rules
And guidelines for the fool

KINGS OF KRYPTONITE

After all my progress in self, in conquering fear
I hesitate at the end of the chapter
Reluctant to turn the page
I fear death
Death of the old life and beginning the new
When I should be rejoicing in death
Leaving the old life in the grave
What idiotic nostalgia holds me to the past?
I need to kill the past and give birth to the future
It's not murder; it's a mercy killing
The trimming of fat that benefits the body
The life, the self,
And to all the things that will no longer be…

I bid you farewell.

INDEX OF TITLES

INDEX OF TITLES